Learn to Quilt
With Leather™

Designs by Patricia Converse

HOUSE of
WHITE
BIRCHES
PUBLISHERS
SINCE 1947

D1569327

Quilt Notes

The loves of sewing, quilting and leather have come together in this book. Leather offers new textural and tactile experiences for home sewing. The leather itself inspires designs. Traditional patchwork takes on a new look and feel when stitched in the lap quilt Navajo Lightning. Appliqué is easy because edges do not need to be turned under and because sharp points and curves are easily accomplished. Reverse appliqué and foundation piecing are also easy to accomplish with leather for the same reasons.

Decorative machine and free-motion quilting require only basic skills to yield successful results.

Lightweight leathers are easily sewn on a home sewing machine. Suede is primarily used in this book because the texture and hand are so appealing. Washable suede and leather are now becoming available, making them an elegant choice for home-decorating projects. Some care must be taken to work with the characteristics of leather. This book offers practical tips, clear instructions and patterns for over a dozen projects. The techniques for working with suede can be transferred to projects of your own design inspired by the projects found here.

Table of Contents

General Instructions

Quilting with leather is a bit different than quilting with fabrics. Be sure to practice all techniques on samples before working on a project.

Purchasing Leather. Leather is sold by the square foot. A pigskin suede skin averages about 12 square feet, but not all pigs are the same size. If visiting a store, take a tape measure with you to be sure the pieces needed can be cut from the skin available. When ordering online, remember large pieces must be cut from the center, skins are irregular in shape and the square footage includes the entire skin. Do not order your skins too small.

Grain & Nap. The grain of leather runs down the backbone of the skin. There is less stretch lengthwise on a skin. Long pieces should be cut lengthwise on skins when possible. There is a nap on suede. Pieces should be cut with a consistent nap. To check the nap, run your hand along the piece. In one direction, it feels smooth and in the opposite direction, it feels rough. The smooth side is with the nap, and the rough side is against the nap.

Piecing to Make a Larger Piece of Leather. Occasionally, the leather available is not the proper size for a large piece. Think about where a seam would be most pleasing to create a larger piece. If using suede, keep the nap consistent in both pieces. Cut straight edges on rough oversized pieces, overlap, glue-baste and topstitch with matching thread. Cut the large piece required from the stitched piece.

Marking. Always mark leather on the wrong side. A ballpoint pen works well for marking directly on leather. A fine-tip permanent marker can be used to trace tissue-paper patterns onto the wrong side of the leather. The marker will bleed through the paper eliminating the need to cut out the patterns before marking.

Cutting. A rotary cutter, ruler and cutting mat work very well for suede. If they are not available, fabric shears will work. Always cut leather in a single layer.

Sewing Machine. A home sewing machine will work for sewing lightweight leather. Make sure the machine is in good working order.

Needles. Use a size 14–16 leather needle for machine sewing. The leather needle is very sharp and will cut through the leather. A size 18 denim needle works for some applications. For hand sewing, a triangular tipped glover's needle is best. An awl can be used to pierce holes if needed.

Stitching. A stitch length of 7–10 stitches per inch is recommended, as tight stitches will tear the leather. Longer stitch lengths are attractive for quilting. Always test stitching for proper tension on scraps. Never backstitch seams; this tears the leather. Hand-tie off seams.

Thread. Cotton-covered polyester or polyester thread is recommended. All-purpose or size 50 thread is a good choice for seams. Heavy duty, size 28-weight topstitching thread can be used for quilting or decorative stitching as desired. Use a longer stitch length with heavy threads.

Pins. Dressmaking pins will not work for pinning leather, as they make holes and are hard to work. Paper clips and binding clips can be easily used to hold the leather layers together. Safety pins can be used for pin basting the quilt sandwich by inserting the pin tips directly through the seam line.

Seams. Seams in leather can only be stitched once; leather is weakened by the holes, and the holes are permanent. The seam allowance for this pattern book is ¼" unless otherwise noted.

Plain seams can be held together for stitching with paper clips instead of straight pins as shown in Figure 1. Finger-press plain seams open. After finger pressing, the seam can sit under the weight of books to further press it. A clean rolling pin can also be used for pressing.

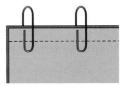

Figure 1
Plain seams are held together
with paper clips for sewing.

Lap seams are constructed by overlapping the ends of the strips ¼" as shown in Figure 2. Glue-baste and topstitch with one or more rows of stitching.

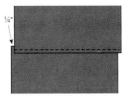

Figure 2
Overlap ends of strips
¼" and stitch as shown.

Glue. Rubber cement is the most commonly used glue. Quilter's Choice Basting Glue is another good choice, as it can easily be applied in very small amounts. Both dry quickly and make it easy to hold small pieces in place for sewing to help seams open and flat after stitching. Where specific glue is noted, it is considered best for the application. Be careful not to smear the glue or rubber cement onto the front side of the pieces as it will leave a stain.

Interfacing. Fusible interfacing is sometimes used with leather for stability. The interfacing also helps the leather to slide on the machine throat plate. Always make a test sample to check for heat damage before adhering interfacing to leather for a project.

Shrink interfacing if recommended by the manufacturer. Check interfacing for stretch. Most interfacing has less stretch along the length.

Cut ½" strips along the length of the interfacing. These strips will be adhered to the wrong side of long seams for stability. The manufacturer often recommends the interfacing be adhered using a damp press cloth. When working on leather, the steam from the damp press cloth is likely to damage and/or shrink the leather. Use a dry press cloth to protect the leather. The dry heat will only make a temporary bond. This temporary bond is acceptable, as the interfacing will be stitched in place when seams are stitched.

Walking Foot or Even-Feed Foot. This foot is very helpful for seams and for quilting because it keeps the layers from sliding. This foot is used on all projects unless otherwise noted.

Stabilizer—Removable or Paper. If the feed dogs are marring the leather when stitching or the leather is not sliding well on the throat plate, place tissue paper or removable stabilizer between the machine and the project. Remove the backing after stitching.

Caring for Leather. Washable suede is now available for home sewing. If washable suede is used, follow the manufacturer's recommendations for care. A suede brush or stone can be used to clean the surface of suede. Dry cleaning using a special process for suede and leather can be done by a reputable dry cleaner.

Inserting Zippers. All the pillows in this book have zippers on the backside opening. The zippers allow for easy removal of the cover for washing or dry cleaning. The lapped application found on the zipper packaging is suitable for the fabrics used for pillow backing. Special instructions for adding a zipper to leather are also included in the zipper packaging.

Making Pillows. To adapt pillow patterns to another size pillow, measure across the pillow form from seam to seam; add a seam allowance. Make a sample pillow cover to check size.

Basic Sewing Tools & Supplies Needed. The following is a list of basic tools and supplies needed to sew with leather: sewing machine; walking foot or even-feed foot; leather sewing-machine needles size 14 or 16; cotton-covered polyester or polyester; general purpose or 50-weight thread; paper clips; safety pins; basting glue; rotary cutter, mat and ruler; sharp shears; ¾" masking tape; tracing paper; white tissue paper (gift-wrapping type); pencil; ballpoint pen; and fine-tip permanent marker. ■

Navajo Lightning

Capture the wild beauty of a desert thunderstorm with this tri-tone quilt.

Project Specifications
Skill Level: Intermediate
Quilt Size: 42½" x 63¾"
Block Size: 10⅝" x 10⅝"
Number of Blocks: 24

Fabric & Batting
- 12 square feet gold suede
- 18 square feet rust suede
- 24 square feet brown suede
- 2¼ yards 45"-wide backing fabric
- Batting 44" x 63"

Supplies & Tools
- All-purpose thread to match suede
- Brown and gold 28-weight topstitching thread
- 2 yards 22"-wide removable fabric stabilizer
- 1 yard fusible interfacing
- Basic sewing tools and supplies (see pages 4 & 5)

Instructions
Note: *A ¼" seam allowance is used throughout. Use walking foot for all sewing. Press seams open after stitching referring to the General Instructions.*

Cutting
1. Cut one each rust and gold suede and two brown suede rectangles 16" x 24".

2. Cut two 16" x 24" pieces of removable fabric stabilizer. Cut remainder into 1"-wide strips.

A Block
10⅝" x 10⅝" Block

A Block Reversed
10⅝" x 10⅝" Block

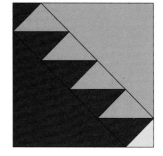

B Block
10⅝" x 10⅝" Block

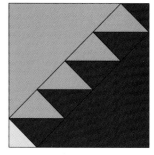

B Block Reversed
10⅝" x 10⅝" Block

3. Cut (12) 9⅜" x 9⅜" squares brown suede; cut each square on one diagonal to make C triangles.

4. Cut (12) 3" x 3" squares brown suede; cut each square on one diagonal to make 24 D triangles.

5. Cut six 9⅜" x 9⅜" squares each rust and gold; cut each square in half on one diagonal to make 12 each rust (E) and gold (F) triangles.

6. Cut six 3" x 3" squares each rust and gold; cut each square in half on one diagonal to make 12 each rust (G) and gold (H) triangles.

7. Cut a 44" x 63" backing piece and an 8" x 40" hanging sleeve strip from backing fabric.

8. Cut 1½"-wide strips of rust suede to make a 230" length for binding.

Piecing the Blocks

1. Lay out one each brown and gold rectangles with right sides together; tape to the surface. Draw a grid of 24 squares measuring 3⅞" x 3⅞" with a pen or fine-tip permanent marker on the wrong side of the gold as shown Figure 1.

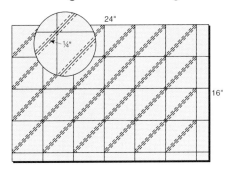

Figure 1
Draw a grid of 24 squares measuring 3⅞" x 3⅞"
on the wrong side of the gold. Draw diagonal
lines through square corners; measure ¼" from
each line and draw dashed lines.

2. Draw diagonal lines from corner to corner through squares; measure ¼" from each line and draw dashed lines, again referring to Figure 1.

3. Remove from table and place stabilizer piece on the underside; stitch on the dashed lines. Cut apart on the solid lines as shown in Figure 2.

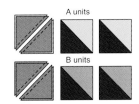

Figure 2
Cut apart on the solid lines and
open to create A and B units.

4. Open each resulting triangle and finger-press seams open. You will need 48 brown/gold A triangle units. Repeat with the brown and rust pieces to make 48 brown/rust B triangle units.

5. Referring to Figure 3, join four A units; add a C triangle to the dark side and an F triangle to the light side of the A unit. Add D to one corner and G to the opposite corner to complete one A Block; repeat for six blocks. **Note:** *If the seams are not feeding through the machine smoothly, place 1" stabilizer strips under the stitching area. This should allow the leather to slide more easily on the throat plate of the machine.*

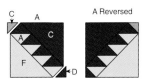

Figure 3
Complete A and A Reversed
Blocks as shown.

6. Complete six A Reversed Blocks, again referring to Figure 3.

7. Referring to Figure 4, join four B units; add a C triangle to the dark side and an E triangle to the light side of the B unit. Add H to one corner and D to the remaining corner to complete one B Block; repeat for six blocks.

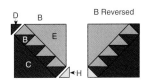

Figure 4
Complete B and B Reversed
Blocks as shown.

8. Complete six B Reversed Blocks, again referring to Figure 4.

9. Apply fusible interfacing to the wrong side of all seams for stability referring to Interfacing on page 5.

Completing the Quilt

1. Lay out the stitched blocks in six rows of four blocks each referring to Figure 5; join the blocks in rows. Join the rows to complete the pieced top.

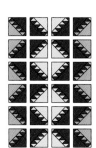

Figure 5
Lay out the stitched blocks
in 6 rows of 4 blocks.

2. Lay the backing on a flat surface right side down; smooth and tape to surface slightly taut using ¾"-wide masking tape.

3. Center the batting on top of the backing; smooth and tape. Center the quilt top right side up on the batting aligning edges with backing; smooth and tape to surface. **Note:** *Be careful not to stretch the leather.*

4. Pin-baste layers together placing pins in the ditch of seams; do not close pins. Pin-baste at edges within the ¼" seam allowance.

5. To mark parallel lines on the quilt top for quilting, place masking tape on the top in a zigzag design as shown in Figure 6.

Figure 6
Place masking tape on the
top in a zigzag design.

6. Using the 28-weight topstitching thread, stitch close to the edge of the masking tape using gold on the brown and brown on the gold and rust sections. Stitch slowly and carefully through all layers on each side of the masking tape. Pull thread ends to the backside, knot and sink knots in quilt backing.

7. Remove masking tape.

8. Machine-baste the outer layers of the quilt edges together inside the ¼" seam allowance.

9. To add a hanging sleeve, fold the short ends of the sleeve strip to the wrong side ⅜" and press. Fold ends in again and stitch to hem. Fold the strip along the length with wrong sides together; stitch to make a tube. press with seam on bottom edge.

10. Center sleeve on the top edge of the wrong side of stitched top; machine-baste to the top edge as shown in Figure 7.

Figure 7
Machine-baste the sleeve to the top edge
of the wrong side of the stitched top.

11. Hand-stitch bottom edge of sleeve to the backing.

12. Piece the rust suede binding strips together with lap seams as needed referring to Seams in the General Instructions.

13. Trim backing and batting even with quilt top.

14. Clip the binding to the edge of the quilt top with right sides together and raw edges even; stitch through all layers, mitering corners and overlapping ends as shown in Figure 8.

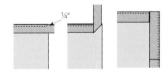

Figure 8
Miter corners; overlap ends.

15. Fold binding to the backside, enclosing raw edges. Glue-baste in place; let glue dry.

16. Topstitch in the ditch of the binding seam from the right side to finish. **Note:** *This stitching should also catch the binding on the backside to hold in place.* ■

Navajo Lightning
Placement Diagram
42½" x 63¾"

Prairie Point Pillow

Prairie points are simple to make when cut from leather.

Project Specifications

Skill Level: Beginner
Pillow Size: 14" x 14" without prairie points

Fabric

- 5 square feet aqua velvet pigskin suede
- 4" x 12" scrap each red, ivory and black velvet pigskin suede

Supplies & Tools

- Aqua all-purpose thread
- ⅜ yard 22"-wide fabric stabilizer
- 14" x 14" pillow form
- 12" matching zipper
- Basic sewing tools and supplies (see pages 4 & 5)

Instructions

1. Cut the following from aqua velvet pigskin suede: two 4½" x 14½" A rectangles; two 4½" x 6½" B rectangles; one 6½" x 6½" C square; two 7¼" x 14½" backing rectangles; and two 1" x 2" zipper tabs.

2. Cut one 3" x 3" square red scrap; cut the square on both diagonals to make four D triangles as shown in Figure 1.

Figure 1
Cut square on both diagonals to make D triangles.

3. Cut two red scrap (E) and four ivory scrap (F) squares 2½" x 2½"; cut each square in half on both diagonals to make eight E and 16 F triangles.

4. Cut three 3" x 3" squares black scrap; cut each square in half on both diagonals to make 12 G triangles.

5. Place one D and two F triangles on opposite right sides of C, overlapping the D triangles with F and leaving ¼" at each end as shown in Figure 2; glue-baste within the seam allowance area. Repeat on the remaining sides of C.

Figure 2
Overlap pieces as shown;
leave ¼" at each end.

6. Cut 1"-wide strips of fabric stabilizer. Clip a strip of fabric stabilizer to one edge on the wrong side of C. Place B right sides together along the stabilized edge of C; clip to hold. Stitch in place with a plain seam as shown in Figure 3.

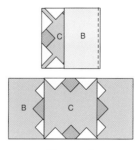

Figure 3
Stitch B to opposite sides of C.

Remove stabilizer; press seam open referring to Seams on page 4. **Note:** *The stabilizer will help the pieces glide over the throat plate when stitching.* Repeat on the opposite side of C.

7. Repeat step 6 with A pieces on opposite sides of the pieced unit as shown in Figure 4.

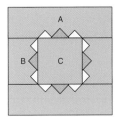

Figure 4
Sew A to the remaining
sides of C.

8. Apply fusible interfacing to the wrong side of all seams for stability referring to Interfacing on page 5.

9. Glue-baste two each E and F and three G triangles to each side of the pieced top, overlapping triangles and leaving ¼" at each end as shown in Figure 5.

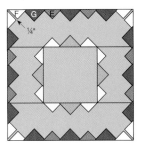

Figure 5
Place triangles on each edge
of the pieced top.

10. Stitch a zipper tab to each end of the zipper to extend the length. Insert zipper between the two backing pieces with tabs under the seam on the 14½" sides following zipper manufacturer's instructions. Trim zippered backing to 14½" x 14½", if necessary.

11. Open zipper. Place pillow top and zipper backing right sides together. Stitch all around using a ¼" seam allowance. Trim corners.

12. Turn right side out though zipper opening; insert pillow form and zip to close. ◼

Prairie Point Pillow
Placement Diagram
14" x 14" (without prairie points)

Autumn Colors

A simple landscape is formed using curved pieces with detail stitching to form tree shapes.

Project Specifications
Skill Level: Intermediate
Wall Quilt Size: 12½" x 10"

Fabric & Batting
- 1 (4½" x 10") rectangle each ivory, rust, gold and red velvet pigskin suede
- 8" x 13" rectangle brown velvet pigskin suede
- 11" x 14" rectangle muslin
- Backing 13½" x 11"
- Batting 13½" x 11"

Supplies & Tools
- Brown 28-weight topstitching thread
- Machine darning foot
- Basic sewing tools and supplies (see pages 4 & 5)

Instructions

1. Trace full-size separate pattern pieces onto white tissue paper.

2. Lay the tissue-paper patterns on the wrong side of the suede pieces as directed on patterns for color; trace over pattern lines with a fine-tip permanent marker. **Note:** *The marker will bleed through the tissue paper onto the suede. Pattern pieces are reversed for tracing.*

3. Cut out suede pieces on traced lines.

4. Cut two 1¾" x 12½" A and two 1¾" x 7" B strips brown suede.

5. Press muslin square and lay flat; lay batting on the muslin.

6. Draw a 12½" x 10" rectangle on the batting with the fine-tip permanent marker. Measure in 1½" from each side and draw an inner rectangle as shown in Figure 1.

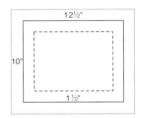

Figure 1
Measure in 1½" from each side and draw an inner rectangle.

7. Place the pieces of colored suede in the inner rectangle right side up in numerical order, overlapping pieces; glue-baste pieces to the batting and to each other at overlapping edges.

8. Lower the feed dogs on your machine, reduce presser-foot pressure and attach a darning foot to your machine. Using brown 28-weight topstitching thread and a constant machine speed, stitch tree shapes onto the glued background surface in a freehand style, using several rows of stitching for the thicker branches and fewer rows for thinner branches. **Note:** *The full-size drawing of the landscape design shows tree stitching lines that may be used as guides to help you stitch your own trees.*

9. Lay the B strips on the stitched landscape short side edges overlapping edges ¼" onto landscape; glue-baste to hold. Stitch ⅛" from inside edge of B.

10. Repeat with the A strips along the top and bottom edges.

11. Trim batting and muslin even with the stitched top.

12. Cut two ½" x 2" hanging tabs from suede scraps. Glue-baste ends in place on the backing piece 1½" from top edge and 3" from side edges as shown in Figure 2. Stitch across each end of each tab.

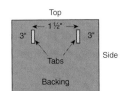

Figure 2
Place tabs 1½" from top edge
and 3" from side edges.

13. Press under ½" all around backing piece.

14. Glue-baste pressed backing to the wrong side of the stitched top; topstitch close to outer edges through all layers to finish. ■

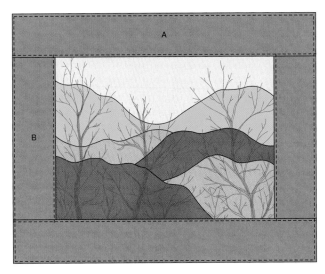

Autumn Colors
Placement Diagram
12½" x 10"

Landscape Pattern

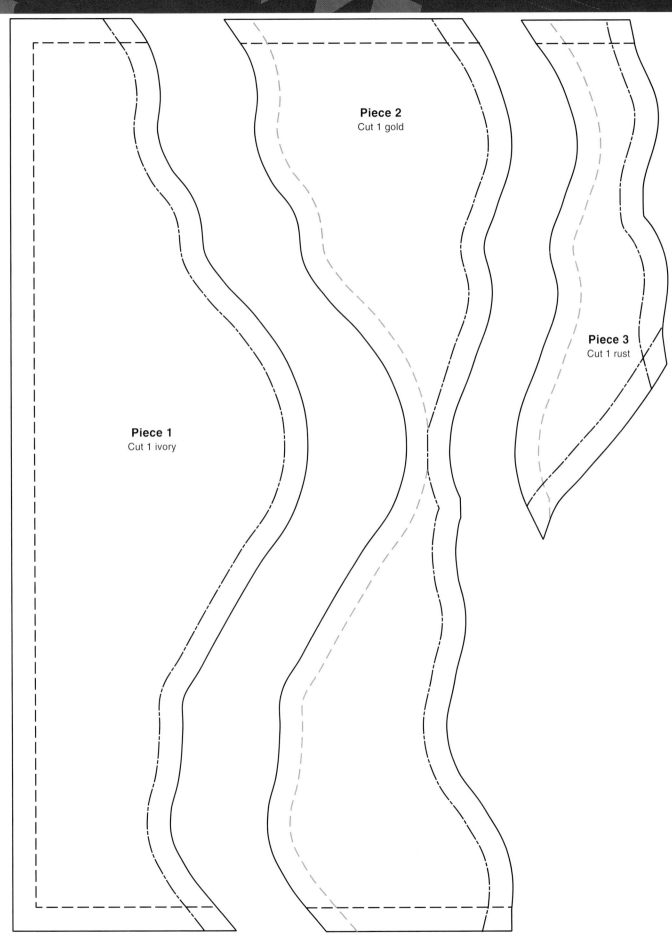

Piece 2
Cut 1 gold

Piece 3
Cut 1 rust

Piece 1
Cut 1 ivory

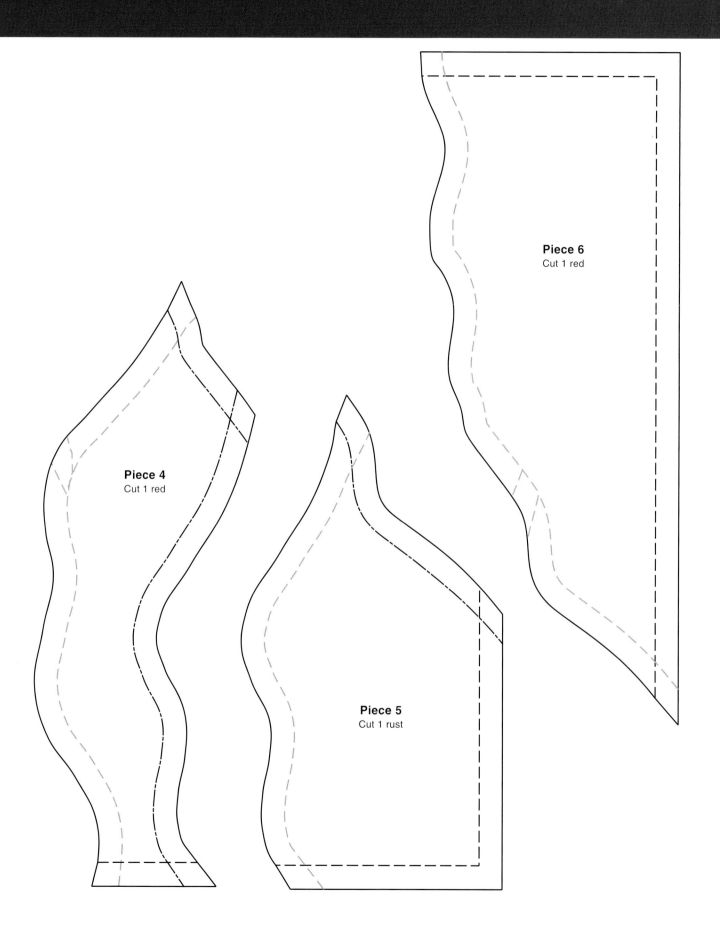

Piece 6
Cut 1 red

Piece 4
Cut 1 red

Piece 5
Cut 1 rust

Black Beauty

The black horse head stands out against the tan foreground in this reverse-appliquéd pillow.

Project Specifications
Skill Level: Intermediate
Pillow Size: 16" x 16"

Fabric & Batting
- 5 square feet ivory velvet pigskin suede
- 1 square foot black velvet pigskin suede

Supplies & Tools
- All-purpose thread to match ivory suede
- 14" ivory zipper
- 16" x 16" pillow form
- 16" x 16" square removable fabric stabilizer
- 5"–6" sharp scissors
- Basic sewing tools and supplies (see pages 4 & 5)

Instructions

1. Press a piece of white tissue paper flat. Trace the horse head pattern onto the tissue paper. Cut out horse head silhouette pattern. **Note:** *The horse head pattern is reversed for tracing onto the wrong side of the suede.*

2. Cut one 10" x 12" rectangle black suede and one 16½" x 16½" square ivory suede.

3. Place the ivory suede square on a table wrong side up. Place the tissue-paper pattern on top of the suede square and align. Using a ballpoint pen, trace over the cutout lines.

4. Using sharp scissors, cut out areas in the ivory suede.

5. Place a piece of scrap paper on a table. Place the ivory suede on the paper with wrong side up. Place a small amount of basting glue near the cutout edges on the wrong side of the ivory suede.

6. Lay the right side of the black suede rectangle down on the glue side of the ivory suede, keeping both layers smooth; let the glue dry.

7. Clip the stabilizer square under the wrong side of the layered pillow top; topstitch along the edges of each cutout area.

8. Pull all beginning and ending threads to the wrong side; knot to secure.

9. Remove the stabilizer.

10. Cut two 8¼" x 16½" rectangles ivory suede for backing and two 1" x 3" strips for zipper tabs.

11. Stitch a tab to each end of the zipper. Insert zipper between the two backing pieces with tabs under the seam on the 16½" sides following zipper manufacturer's instructions. Trim zippered backing to 16½" x 16½", if necessary.

12. Lay the zippered backing right side down on a table; lay the stitched top on top. Glue-baste the edges together. Topstitch ⅛" from edge all around; knot threads and pull to inside of pillow.

13. Insert pillow form to finish. ■

Center

Match on line to make complete pattern

Zipper Backing

Match on line to make complete pattern

Horse Head

Black Beauty
Placement Diagram
16" x 16"

Log Cabin Trio

Use both sides of velvet pigskin suede to add different texture to these pillows made with familiar Log Cabin designs.

Project Notes

Velvet pigskin suede has a suede side and a leather side. The suede side is shown in our illustrations with a darker color and the leather side is shown with a lighter color. Alternating the textures adds interest to the Log Cabin pattern.

The leather strips want to wiggle and wander so foundation piecing is used. This will assure accurate stitching.

Masking tape can be used to hold the suede in place for stitching. Use the tape in place of pins. Place the tape within the seam allowance (on the outer-most edge) to avoid stitching over it or having the tape mark the project.

If pressing is desired, make a sample and test using an iron set on low. Press only from the backside; do not use steam. Use a press cloth or the muslin foundation.

Project Specifications

Skill Level: Intermediate
Pillow Size: 14" x 14"

Fabric & Batting

- 8 square feet each brown and red velvet pigskin suede
- 1 yard muslin
- 1 yard backing fabric

Supplies & Tools

- Brown all-purpose thread
- 3 (14" x 14") pillow forms
- 3 (12") zippers to match backing
- Basic sewing tools and supplies (see pages 4 & 5)

Instructions

Note: A ¼" seam allowance is used throughout. Use walking foot for all sewing. Press seams open after stitching referring to the General Instructions.

1. Cut three muslin squares 16" x 16" for foundations.

2. Cut one 2½" x 2½" square red suede for Courthouse Steps Pillow center, piece 1.

3. Cut remaining red and brown suede into 1½"-wide strips to be used for all pillows.

Courthouse Steps Pillow

1. Use a permanent fine-tip marker to draw the stitching lines onto muslin foundation. The marker should be visible on both sides of the muslin making placement easier.

2. To make the Courthouse Steps Pillow, find the center of one muslin square. Draw a 2" x 2" square in the center. Work out from the center square in 1"-wide strips, drawing the pattern referring to Figure 1; add numbers to the muslin.

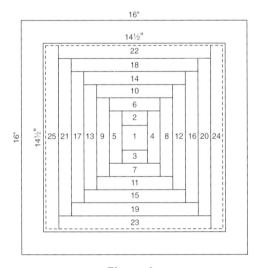

Figure 1
Draw the Courthouse Steps pattern in 1"-wide strips around a 2" center; number as shown.

3. Add a ¼" seam allowance beyond the final marked line.

4. Place the 2½" x 2½" red suede square on the wrong side of the muslin foundation over the piece 1 center square with suede side up.

5. Cut two 2½" pieces of brown suede from 1½"-wide strips for pieces 2 and 3.

6. Place the brown strip, suede side down, along the piece 2 edge of piece 1; tape the pieces in place with masking tape, keeping tape off the stitching line as shown in Figure 2.

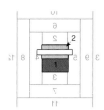

Figure 2
Tape piece 2 to piece 1 on the
unmarked side of the muslin.

7. Turn the project over and stitch on the marked line between pieces 1 and 2, extending stitching ¼" past seam ends as shown in Figure 3.

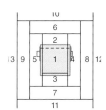

Figure 3
Turn the project over;
stitch on the marked line
between pieces 1 and 2,
extend stitching ¼"
past seam ends.

8. Turn project over, open seam and repeat with a second brown strip for piece 3.

9. Cut two 4½" strips red suede for pieces 4 and 5. Place piece 4 leather side down on the 1-2-3 combination as shown in Figure 4. Tape, turn stitched unit over and stitch on the marked line

between pieces 1-2-3; turn project over, open seam and repeat with piece 5.

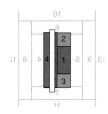

Figure 4
Place piece 4
leather side down
on the 1-2-3
combination.

10. Continue cutting strips to the required size for pieces 6–25, measuring the size required on the muslin foundation and adding ½" for seam allowance.

11. Add strips around the stitched center in numerical order, alternating suede side up with leather side up referring to the Placement Diagram on page 29 for positioning.

12. After all strips have been added, trim excess muslin along the marked line; set aside.

Log Cabin Pillow

1. To make the Log Cabin Pillow, cut one 1½" x 1½" square each brown and red suede for pieces 1 and 2.

Figure 5
Divide the 2" square into two 1"
squares and one 1" x 2" rectangle.

2. Find the center of one muslin square; draw a 2" square in the center. Divide the 2" square into two 1" squares and one 1" x 2" rectangle as shown in Figure 5.

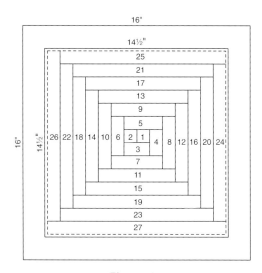

Figure 6
Work out from the center in 1"-wide
strips drawing the pattern and
numbering as shown.

3. Work out from the center in 1"-wide strips to draw the pattern referring to Figure 6; add a ¼" seam allowance all around and add numbers to each strip.

4. Place the red square leather side up over piece 1; sew the pieces to the muslin foundation in numerical order with the leather side up on all even numbered strips and suede side up on all odd-numbered strips, referring to instructions for the Courthouse Steps Pillow until all strips have been added; set aside.

Offset Log Cabin Pillow

1. Center and mark a 14½" x 14½" square on the remaining muslin square. Mark a ¼" seam allowance all around the inside of the marked square. Draw a 1" square in the upper right corner for piece 1 as shown in Figure 7.

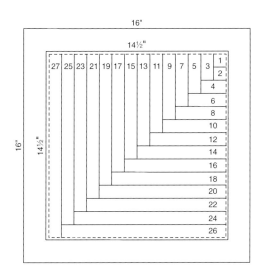

Figure 7
Draw the Offset Log Cabin pattern
and number strips as shown.

2. Draw a second square below piece 1 for piece 2. Draw a 1"-wide rectangle on the left side of pieces 1 and 2 for piece 3. Continue adding 1"-wide rectangles to the muslin for pieces 5–27, again referring to Figure 7.

3. Cut one square each red and brown suede 1½" x 1½".

4. Place the red square suede side up over piece 1. Sew the pieces to the muslin foundation in numerical order, alternating suede and leather sides of the strips and referring to the instructions for the Courthouse Steps Pillow to complete the block; set aside.

Finishing

1. Cut six 8" x 14½" backing pieces.

2. Insert zipper between two backing pieces referring to the instructions provided with the zipper and using a ½" seam allowance.

3. Open zipper. Place pillow top and zipper backing right sides together. Stitch all around using a ¼" seam allowance. Trim corners.

4. Turn right side out though zipper opening; insert pillow form and zip to close. Repeat for all pillows. ■

Courthouse Steps Pillow
Placement Diagram
14" x 14"

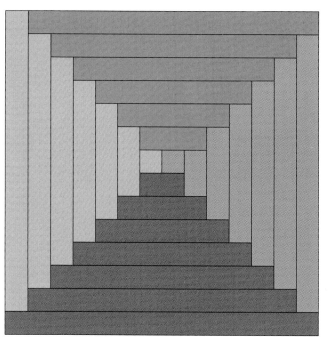

Log Cabin Pillow
Placement Diagram
14" x 14"

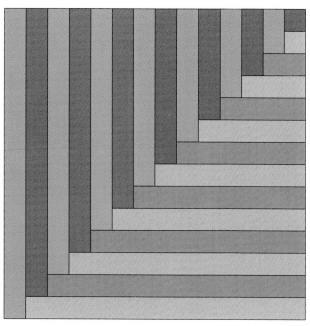

Offset Log Cabin Pillow
Placement Diagram
14" x 14"

Autumn Leaves

Simple leaf shapes are scattered on the top of this pretty pillow.

Project Note
The kidskins used in this project are small so two skins may be needed. Refer to Piecing To Make a Larger Piece on page 3.

Project Specifications
Skill Level: Beginner
Pillow Size: 14" x 14"

Fabric & Batting
- 5 square feet saddle tan doe kidskin
- 3 pieces (1 square foot) red velvet pigskin suede
- ½ yard red or gold backing fabric
- 15" x 15" lightweight batting

Supplies & Tools
- Red, gold and medium brown all-purpose thread
- 15" x 15" square removable fabric stabilizer
- 14" x 14" pillow form
- 12" matching zipper
- 4 brown horsehair tassels
- 5"–6" sharp shears
- Basic sewing tools and supplies (see pages 4 & 5)

Instructions
1. Trace leaf patterns onto paper; cut out on traced lines.

2. Cut a 14½" x 14½" square saddle tan kidskin for background. ***Note:*** *Refer to page 3 if piecing the skin is necessary to result in this size.*

3. Trace three large and three small leaf patterns onto the backside of the red suede using a ballpoint pen. Cut out shapes on traced lines.

4. Arrange the cut leaves on the background square at least ½" from seam allowance. Place basting glue on the backside of each leaf and press onto background with hands.

5. Place the stabilizer square on the backside of the glued background square. With red thread and leather needle, topstitch the leaves onto the background close to edges as shown in Figure 1; pull beginning and ending threads to the backside and knot to secure. Remove stabilizer.

Figure 1
Topstitch the leaves onto the background close to edges.

6. Cut a 15" x 15" lining square from red or gold backing fabric.

7. Sandwich the batting square between the lining square and the stitched top; hold layers together with paper clips.

HOUSE OF WHITE BIRCHES, BERNE, INDIANA 46711   WWW.WHITEBIRCHES.COM

8. Machine straight-stitch the vein and stem lines using medium brown thread and a walking foot. Add extra rows of stitching to make the stem the desired width; pull threads to the backside and knot to secure.

9. Create a branch design referring to Figure 2 for positioning; stitch as in step 8. **Note:** *It is difficult to mark the leather, so it is best to work the design freehand.*

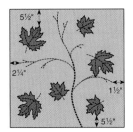

Figure 2
The branch design used
on the sample is shown.

10. Baste the edges of the quilted pillow top together a scant ¼" from edges; trim batting and lining even with the pillow top.

11. Cut 1"-wide strips from remaining saddle tan kidskin; join strips on short ends with lap seams to make a 62" length of cording.

12. Fold the cording strip in half along length with wrong sides together as shown in Figure 3; lightly glue the layers together to hold.

Figure 3
Fold the cording strip in half along
length with wrong sides together.

13. Run a small bead of glue along the outer edges of the quilted pillow top; glue cording piece in place. Measure where cording ends will meet; add a ¼" seam allowance to one end and trim off remainder of cording length. Overlap ends and topstitch to make a lap seam; finish gluing in place.

14. Cut two 8" x 14½" rectangles red or gold backing.

15. Insert zipper between the two backing pieces on the 14½" sides following zipper manufacturer's instructions. Trim zippered backing to 14½" x 14½", if necessary.

16. Open zipper. Place pillow top and zipper backing right sides together. Stitch all around using a ¼" seam allowance. Trim corners.

17. Turn right side out though zipper opening; insert pillow form and zip to close.

18. Hand-stitch a tassel to the backside at each corner to finish. ■

Autumn Leaves
Placement Diagram
14" x 14"

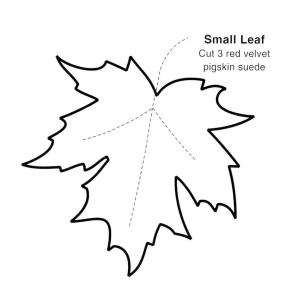

Small Leaf
Cut 3 red velvet
pigskin suede

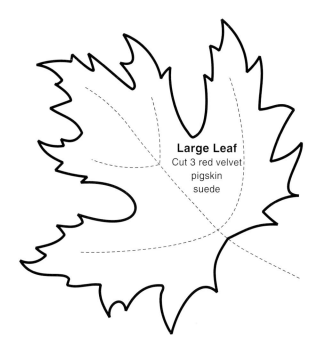

Large Leaf
Cut 3 red velvet
pigskin
suede

Royal Ranch Throw

Keeping warm should be no problem under this comfy leather throw.

Project Specifications
Skill Level: Intermediate
Quilt Size: 50" x 59" (without prairie points)

Fabric & Batting
- 2 square feet ivory velvet pigskin suede
- 14 square feet each forest green, electric blue and purple velvet pigskin suede
- Backing 52" x 61"
- Batting 52" x 61"

Supplies & Tools
- All-purpose thread to match suede
- Gray 28-weight topstitching thread
- ½ yard 22"-wide removable fabric stabilizer
- Basic sewing tools and supplies (see pages 4 & 5)

Instructions
Note: *A ¼" seam allowance is used throughout. Press seams open after stitching referring to the General Instructions.*

Cutting
1. Cut one square ivory suede (A) and two squares each forest green (B), electric blue (C) and purple (D) suedes 4½" x 4½"; cut each square on both diagonals to make four triangles as shown in Figure 1.

Figure 1
Cut squares on both diagonals.

2. Cut (14) 3½" x 3½" E squares ivory suede; cut each square in half on both diagonals to make 54 E triangles.

3. Cut two 10¼" x 50½" forest green F and one each electric blue G and purple H suede strips. Cut one each 10½" x 50½" electric blue I and purple J strips. Fold each strip in half across width and finger-press to mark center.

4. Cut 1"-wide strips removable fabric stabilizer to equal 255".

Piecing the Top
1. Lay out the F, G and H strips on a flat surface as shown in Figure 2.

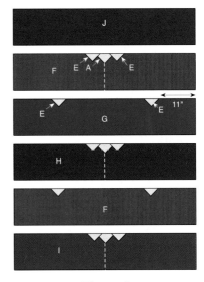

Figure 2
Lay out strips and triangles as shown.

2. Arrange and center one A and two E triangle prairie points on one each F, H and I strips with raw edges even, again referring to Figure 2; align A with center crease and overlap triangles ¼" as shown in Figure 3; glue-baste in place. Let glue dry.

Figure 3
Align A with center
and overlap
triangles ¼".

3. Place an E triangle 11" in from each outer edge on the G and F strips referring to Figure 1; glue-baste in place. Let glue dry.

4. Join the strips in the order arranged to complete the pieced section of the top, clipping stabilizer strips on the wrong side of each seam; remove stabilizer. Press seams open referring to Seams in the General Instructions on page 4.

5. Apply fusible interfacing to the wrong side of all seams for stability referring to Interfacing on page 5.

6. Arrange two each B, C and D triangles with 12 E triangles along each long side of the pieced center, overlapping triangles as necessary as shown in Figure 4 and referring to the Placement Diagram for positioning. Glue-baste in place. Let glue dry.

Figure 4
Arrange triangles,
overlapping as needed.

7. Repeat step 6 with one C, two each B and D and 10 E triangles on the top and bottom of the pieced center, again referring to the Placement Diagram for positioning.

Finishing the Quilt

1. Lay the batting on a flat surface; smooth and lightly tape with masking tape. Lay the backing right side up on the batting; smooth and tape. Lay the quilt top right side down on the backing; smooth and tape.

2. Trim backing and batting to the same size as the quilt top; paper-clip edges together. Remove tape.

3. Stitch all around edges, leaving a 10" opening on one side. Stitch the prairie points in the opening in place to secure. Clip corners; turn right side out through opening.

4. Hand-stitch the backing to the quilt top at the opening. **Note:** *Hand-stitch to the stitching line for prairie points to avoid stitching through the leather.*

5. Lay out the quilt on a flat surface; pull it lightly taut and tape in place. Safety-pin baste layers together, placing pins in the ditch of seams where the holes will be stitched over later; do not close safety pins.

6. Stitch in the ditch of all seams and around outside edges of the top; pull threads to the backside, knot and sink knots in the backing to finish. ◼

Royal Ranch Throw
Placement Diagram
50" x 59" (without prairie points)

Reverse Appliqué Starburst

Use your sewing machine's fancy stitches to try reverse appliqué.

Project Specifications
Skill Level: Intermediate
Pillow Size: 14" x 14"

Fabric & Batting
- 2 square feet red velvet pigskin suede
- 4 square feet gray velvet pigskin suede

Supplies & Tools
- Gray all-purpose thread
- Black 28-weight topstitching thread
- 12" zipper
- 14" x 14" pillow form
- ½ yard 22"-wide removable fabric stabilizer
- 5"–6" sharp scissors
- Basic sewing tools and supplies (see pages 4 & 5)

Instructions
1. Press a piece of white tissue paper flat. Trace the ¼ pillow pattern onto the tissue paper; repeat tracing using edge lines on pattern to align as you trace as shown in Figure 1. Cut out design areas.

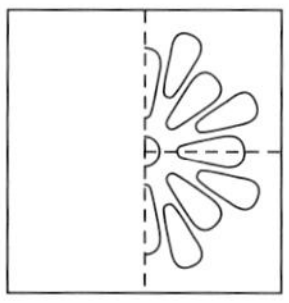

Figure 1
Align pattern
edges to trace.

2. Cut one 13½" x 13½" square red suede and one 14" x 14" square gray suede.

3. Place the gray suede square on a table wrong side up. Place the tissue paper pattern on top of the suede square and align. Using a fine-tip permanent marker, trace over the cutout lines.

4. Using sharp scissors, cut out design areas on the gray suede.

5. Place a piece of scrap paper on a table. Place the gray suede on the paper with wrong side up. Place a small amount of basting glue near the cutout edges on the wrong side of the gray suede.

6. Lay the right side of the red suede down on the glue side of the gray suede, keeping both layers smooth; let the glue dry.

7. Cut a 14" x 14" square fabric stabilizer; clip under the wrong side of the layered pillow top; topstitch along the edges of each cutout area using black 28-weight topstitching thread and decorative machine stitches. **Note:** *The sample shown uses straight, buttonhole and starburst machine-embroidery stitches. A scallop stitch was used to highlight the center area.*

8. Pull all beginning and ending threads to the wrong side; knot to secure.

9. Remove the stabilizer.

10. Cut two 8" x 14½" rectangles gray suede for backing and two 1" x 3" strips for zipper tabs.

11. Stitch a zipper tab to each end of the zipper to extend length. Insert zipper between the two backing pieces on the 14½" sides following zipper manufacturer's instructions. Trim zippered backing to 14½" x 14½", if necessary.

12. Lay the zippered backing right side down on a table; lay the stitched top on top. Glue-baste the edges together. Topstitch ⅛" from edge all around; knot threads and pull to inside of pillow.

13. Insert pillow form to finish. ■

Reverse Appliqué Starburst
Placement Diagram
14" x 14"

¼ **Starburst Pattern**

Amish Inspiration

This leather wall quilt with bold colors and simple lines was inspired by the Amish style.

Project Note

Before cutting, it may be helpful to draw the pieces on the backside of the suede with a ball-point pen. This will help with the placement of the pieces.

Project Specifications

Skill Level: Intermediate
Quilt Size: 38" x 38"

Fabric & Batting

- 7 square feet red velvet pigskin suede
- 8 square feet pewter gray velvet pigskin suede
- 12 square feet electric blue velvet pigskin suede
- 1½ yards 45"-wide backing fabric
- Batting 42" x 42"

Supplies & Tools

- Gray all-purpose thread
- Gray 28-weight topstitching thread
- Toothpick
- ½ yard fusible interfacing
- ½ yard 22"-wide removable fabric stabilizer
- Basic sewing tools and supplies (see pages 4 & 5)

Instructions

Note: *A ¼" seam allowance is used throughout. Press seams open after stitching referring to the General Instructions.*

Cutting

1. Cut one 9½" x 9½" A square and four 8" x 23½" G strips electric blue suede.

2. Cut four 3½" x 3½" F squares, four 8" x 8" H squares and two 9⅜" x 9⅜" D squares red suede. Cut each D square in half on one diagonal to make four D triangles.

3. Cut two 2" x 9½" B strips, two 2" x 12½" C strips and four 3½" x 17½" E strips pewter gray suede. Cut and piece four 2" x 42" strips pewter gray suede for binding.

4. Cut 1"-wide strips removable fabric stabilizer to equal 350".

5. Cut a 42" x 42" backing piece and an 8" x 36" hanging sleeve strip from backing fabric.

Piecing the Top

1. Referring to Seams on page 4, sew B to opposite sides of A with a plain seam, clipping stabilizer on the wrong side of each seam. Add C to the remaining sides.

2. Sew a D triangle to each side of the A-B-C unit.

3. Sew an E strip to opposite sides of the pieced center. Sew F to each end of each remaining E strip. Sew the E-F strips to the remaining sides of the pieced center.

4. Sew G to opposite sides of the pieced center. Sew H to each end of each remaining G strip. Sew a G-H strip to the remaining sides of the pieced center to complete the pieced top. Remove all fabric stabilizer.

5. Apply fusible interfacing to the wrong side of all seams for stability referring to Interfacing on page 5.

Quilting

1. Lay the backing piece on a flat surface with wrong side up; smooth and tape to the surface with masking tape. Center batting on the backing, smooth and tape. Center quilt top right side up on the batting aligned with the backing; smooth and tape to surface. **Note:** *Be careful not to stretch the leather.*

2. Pin-baste with safety pins. **Note:** *Insert ends of pins into the ditch of seams to avoid making holes in the leather. Leave pins open. Pin-baste the outer edges within the ¼" seam allowance.*

3. Trace quilting patterns onto tissue paper; trace each pattern the number of times it will be used.

Tip
When tracing multiple copies of the quilting pattern, stack sheets of tissue paper and trace pattern with a fine-tip permanent marker. The marker will bleed through and mark more than one layer at a time.

4. Center the tissue-paper pattern for the center quilting design on A; tape in place. Using the 28-weight gray topstitching thread, stitch along the lines on the tissue paper through all layers; pull beginning and ending threads to the backside and knot to secure. Remove paper.

5. Repeat step 4 with the heart quilting design in the D triangles, the E-F design on the E strips and F squares and the border quilting design on the G strips and H squares referring to the Placement Diagram for positioning of designs.

6. Machine-baste the outer edges of the quilt together a scant ¼" from edge.

Finishing

1. To add a hanging sleeve, fold the short ends of the sleeve strip to the wrong side ⅜" and press. Fold ends in again and stitch to hem. Fold the strip along the length with wrong sides together; stitch to make a tube. press with seam on bottom edge.

2. Center sleeve on the wrong side top edge of the stitched top and machine-baste in place as shown in Figure 1.

Figure 1
Baste sleeve to the wrong side of
top edge, matching raw edges.

3. Measure in 1" from outer edges of the quilt top; run the pointed end of a toothpick along the ruler to make a temporary line on the quilt top.

4. Measure the length of the sides of the quilt; cut two strips gray binding from binding strips this length.

5. Place a small amount of basting glue on the wrong side of one long edge of a gray binding strip. Glue binding to the quilt top along the toothpick-marked line; let glue dry. Repeat on opposite edge of quilt.

6. Fold binding around the raw edges to the backside of the quilt and glue in place. Topstitch binding in place from the right side through all layers.

7. Repeat with binding strips along the remaining sides with binding strips extending all the way to each end, enclosing the previously stitched binding ends as shown in Figure 2; stitch. Repeat to place a second line of stitching along binding strips.

Figure 2
Overlap binding
strips at ends.

8. Hand-stitch bottom edge and ends of sleeve to backing. ■

Amish Inspiration
Placement Diagram
38" x 38"

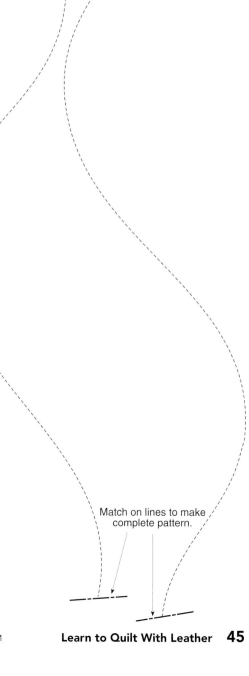

**E-F Quilting
Design**
Trace 4

Match on lines to make
complete pattern.

Center Quilting Design
Trace 1

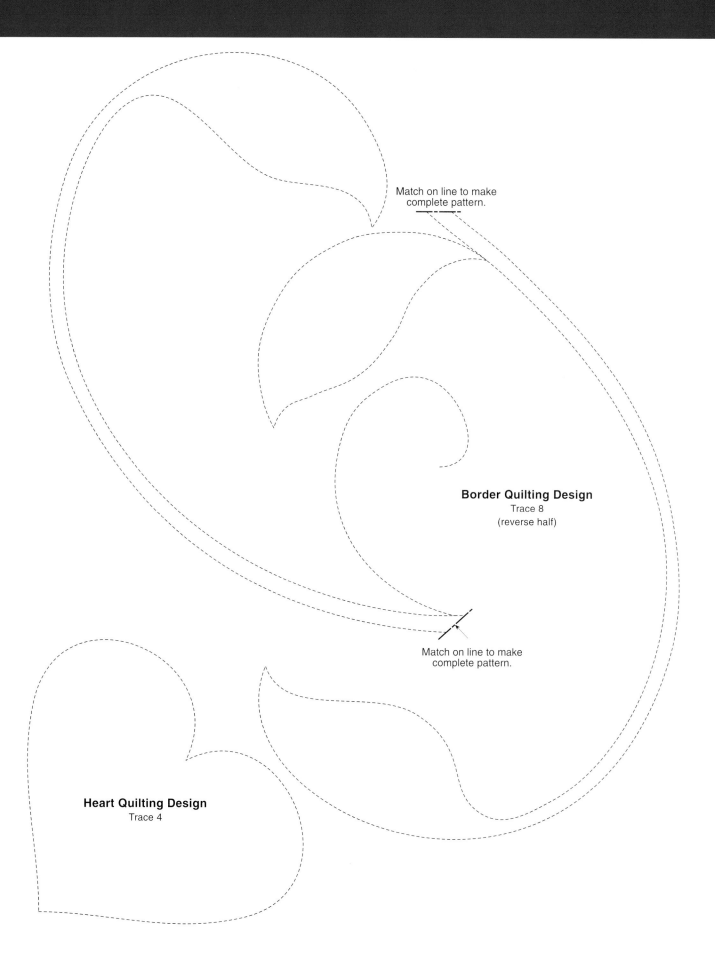

Match on line to make
complete pattern.

Border Quilting Design
Trace 8
(reverse half)

Match on line to make
complete pattern.

Heart Quilting Design
Trace 4

Winter Evergreens

Intricate appliqué is easy when using velvet pigskin suede.

Project Specifications
Skill Level: Intermediate
Quilt Size: 50" x 50"

Fabric & Batting
- 12 square feet ivory velvet pigskin suede
- 27 square feet green velvet pigskin suede
- Backing 51" x 51"
- Batting 50" x 50"

Supplies & Tools
- Ivory and green all-purpose thread
- 2⅛ yards 22"-wide removable fabric stabilizer
- Basic sewing tools and supplies (see page 5)

Instructions
Preparing & Cutting Pieces
1. Trace the pattern for the center medallion onto white tissue paper referring to the drawing given with the pattern for joining the pieces to make the pattern.

2. Cut the pattern out along the marked cutting lines.

3. Draw a 22" x 22" square on the wrong side of the green suede; divide this square into four 11" x 11" squares as shown in Figure 1.

Figure 1
Divide square into (4)
11" x 11" squares.

4. Using the traced squares as guides for positioning, trace one tree pattern onto the wrong side of the green suede using a ballpoint pen; repeat to trace one pattern in each square referring to Figure 2.

Figure 2
Trace 1 pattern
in each square.

5. Cut out tree medallion shape on marked lines.

6. Trace the pattern for the corner tree shape onto white tissue paper referring to the drawing given with the pattern.

7. Cut the pattern out along the marked cutting lines and trace four patterns onto the wrong side of the green suede.

8. Cut out corner tree shapes.

9. Cut one 22½" x 22½" square ivory suede.

10. Cut two of each of the following from green suede: 3" x 22½", 3" x 28", 6" x 19½", 6" x 19¼", 6" x 25" and 6" x 25¼". **Note:** *Refer to page 3 for piecing strips to create longer lengths, if necessary.*

11. Cut two each 5½" x 28½" and 5½" x 38½" strips ivory suede.

12. Cut four 13" x 13" squares and one 22" x 22" square removable fabric stabilizer.

Piecing the Top

1. Lay the cutout tree medallion piece on a piece of paper on a flat surface wrong side up; place basting glue on the entire surface.

2. Lay the right side of the ivory square onto the glued side of the tree piece, centering tree piece; let glue dry.

3. Clip the 22" removable fabric stabilizer square to the wrong side of the glued center square.

4. Topstitch close to all edges of the tree piece using green all-purpose thread; remove fabric stabilizer. **Note:** *The sewing machine needle can become sticky when topstitching and skip stitches. To avoid this, clean needle periodically with a scrap of fabric.*

5. Make a border square using the 3" x 22½" and 3" x 28" green suede strips as shown in Figure 3; **Note:** *The shorter pieces have a ¼" seam to lap under the longer pieces.* Lap the seams and topstitch, again referring to Figure 3.

6. Lay the border square on top of the center square, overlapping as necessary; glue-baste to hold in place. Topstitch lapped seams in place.

7. Use the 5½" x 28½" and 5½" x 38½" strips ivory to make a square as in step 5; lap seams and topstitch.

8. Glue-baste corner tree shape to each corner of the ivory square, aligning inside edge of shape with inside edge of square. Clip a 13" square of stabilizer behind each corner unit; topstitch in place as in step 4. Remove fabric stabilizer.

9. Lay the center square on the stitched ivory square, overlapping as necessary; glue-baste to hold. Topstitch in place.

10. To make green outer border, lap-seam a 19¼" strip on top of a 19½" strip to make a 38½" strip; repeat for two strips.

Figure 3
Lap the seams
and topstitch.

11. Lap-seam a 25" strip on top of a 25¼" strip to make a 50" strip; repeat for two strips.

12. Create a border square as in step 5.

13. Lay the border square on top of the previously stitched center, overlapping pieces; glue-baste to hold. Topstitch in place.

Finishing the Quilt

1. Lay the backing square wrong side up on a flat surface; lay the prepared batting on top. Fold the backing edges over the batting as shown in Figure 4; press. Stitch backing and batting layers together all around edges.

Figure 4
Fold the backing
edges over the batting.

2. Lay the backing/batting layers with batting side up on a flat surface; lay the quilt top on the batting. Smooth all layers; glue-baste to hold.

3. Stitch in the ditch of all seams and ¼" from outer edge. Add a second line of stitching close to the first line all around the outer edge to finish. ◾

Winter Evergreens
Placement Diagram
50" x 50"

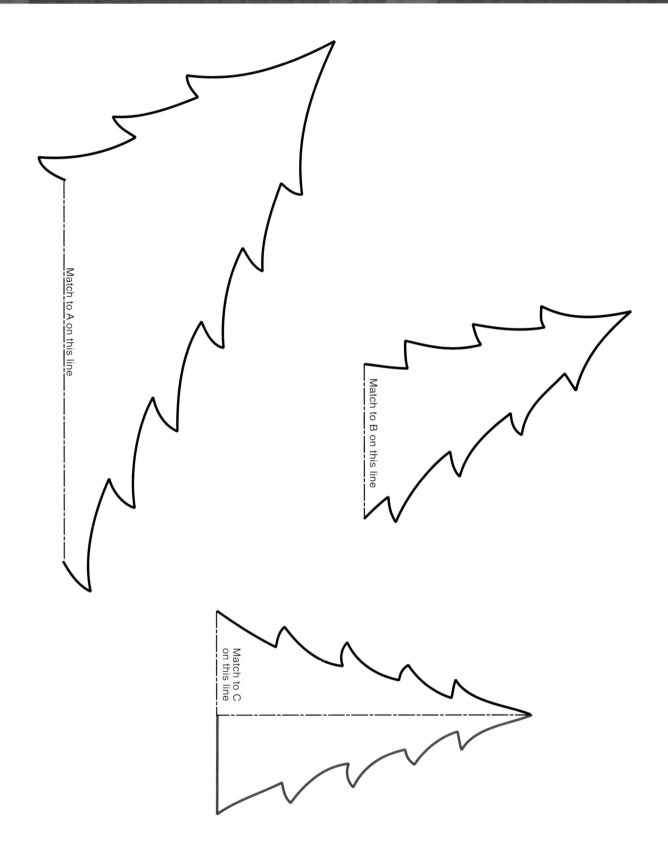

Match to A on this line

Match to B on this line

Match to C on this line

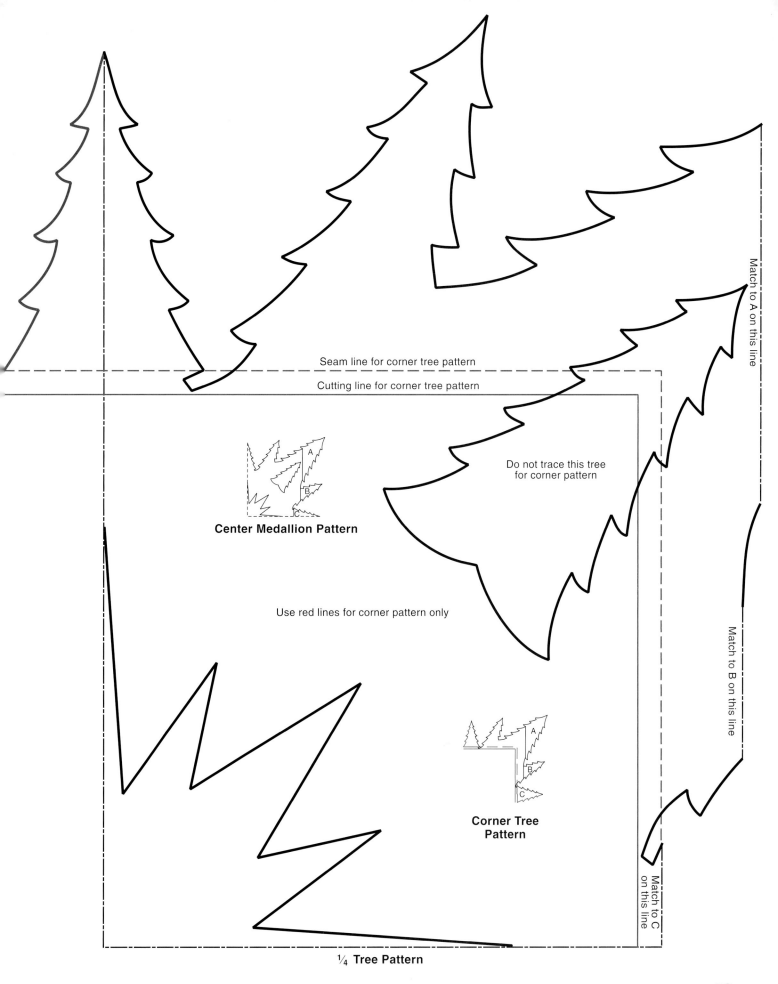

Seam line for corner tree pattern

Cutting line for corner tree pattern

Center Medallion Pattern

Do not trace this tree
for corner pattern

Use red lines for corner pattern only

**Corner Tree
Pattern**

Match to A on this line

Match to B on this line

Match to C
on this line

¼ **Tree Pattern**

Western Nights

Black leather with a silver concho button gives this round, ruffled pillow a Western look.

Project Specifications
Skill Level: Intermediate
Pillow Size: 14" Diameter without ruffle

Fabric & Batting
- 7 square feet black doe kidskin
- 18" x 18" square muslin
- ½ yard black backing fabric
- 18" x 18" lightweight batting

Supplies & Tools
- Black all-purpose thread
- Silver/gray 28-weight topstitching thread
- 12" zipper
- 1½" silver concho or button
- 14" round pillow form
- Basic sewing tools and supplies (see page 5)

Instructions
1. Trace the round pillow pattern onto white tissue paper as shown in Figure 1, adding quilting lines to pattern. Trace the ruffle pattern onto white tissue paper.

Figure 1
Make complete pillow pattern as shown.

2. Lay the pillow pattern on the right side of the kidskin; hold in place with weights if necessary. Cut out pillow shape; repeat to cut one muslin pillow shape.

3. Repeat with ruffle pattern to cut four ruffle pieces.

4. Lay the muslin right side down; place the batting on the muslin. Place the pillow top right side up on top of the batting. Place the tissue paper pattern right side up on the pillow top; use paper clips to hold the layers together.

5. Machine-baste the layers together around the outer edge using a scant ¼" seam allowance.

6. After testing stitch sizes on scraps, stitch the quilting pattern through all layers using the silver/gray 28-weight topstitching thread. When starting and stopping, pull the threads to the backside and knot to secure. Tear paper away.

7. Sew the 1½" silver concho or button to the center of the pillow top.

8. Join ruffle pieces by overlapping seams ¼"; glue. Starting at the inner edge, stitch out to outer edge, turn, take one stitch along outer edge, turn and stitch back to the inner edge as shown in Figure 2.

Figure 2
Join ruffle pieces with lap seams.

HOUSE OF WHITE BIRCHES, BERNE, INDIANA 46711   WWW.WHITEBIRCHES.COM

9. Fold pillow top in half twice to mark centers. Place ruffle right sides together with pillow top, matching the centers on pillow top with the seams on the ruffle; clip to hold.

10. Machine baste the ruffle to the pillow top within the seam allowance.

11. Fold pillow pattern in half. Cut two backing pieces using the folded half pillow pattern, adding ½" to the straight edge as shown in Figure 3.

12. Insert zipper between the straight edges of the two backing pieces referring to the instructions provided with the zipper and using a ½" seam allowance.

13. Open zipper. Place pillow top and zipper backing right sides together. Stitch all around using a ¼" seam allowance. Trim corners.

14. Turn right side out though zipper opening; insert pillow form and zip to close. ■

Figure 3
Cut backing pieces, adding a ½" seam allowance to the straight edge as shown.

Western Nights
Placement Diagram
14" Diameter (without ruffle)

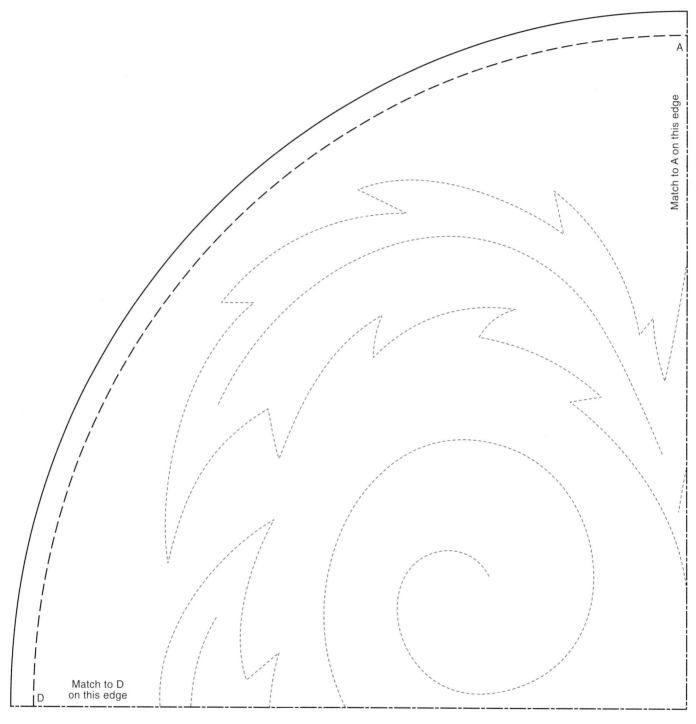

Match to D
on this edge

D

Pillow 1

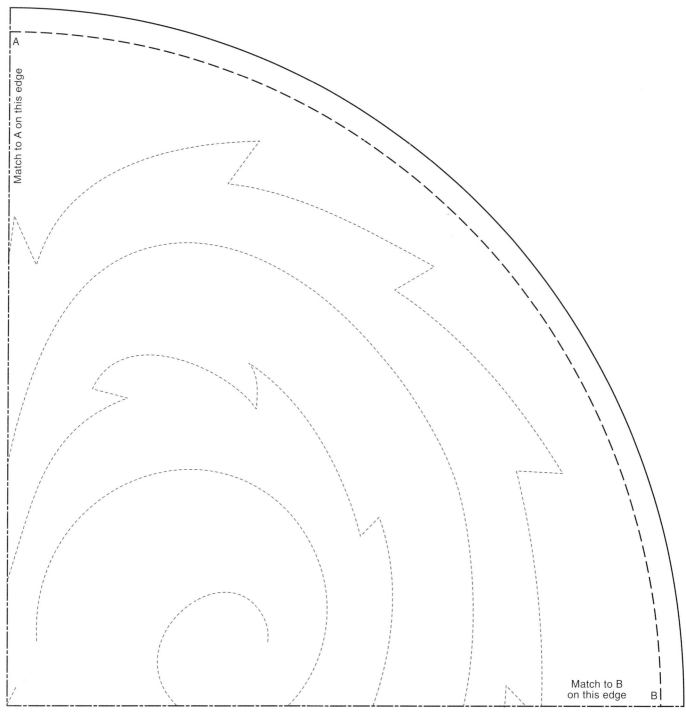

A

Match to A on this edge

Match to B
on this edge

B

Pillow 2

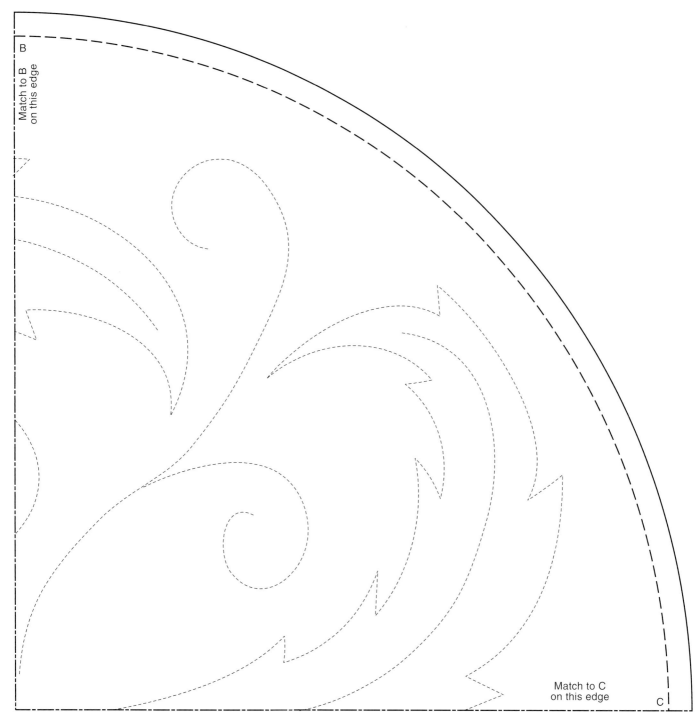

B

Match to B
on this edge

Match to C
on this edge

C

Pillow 3

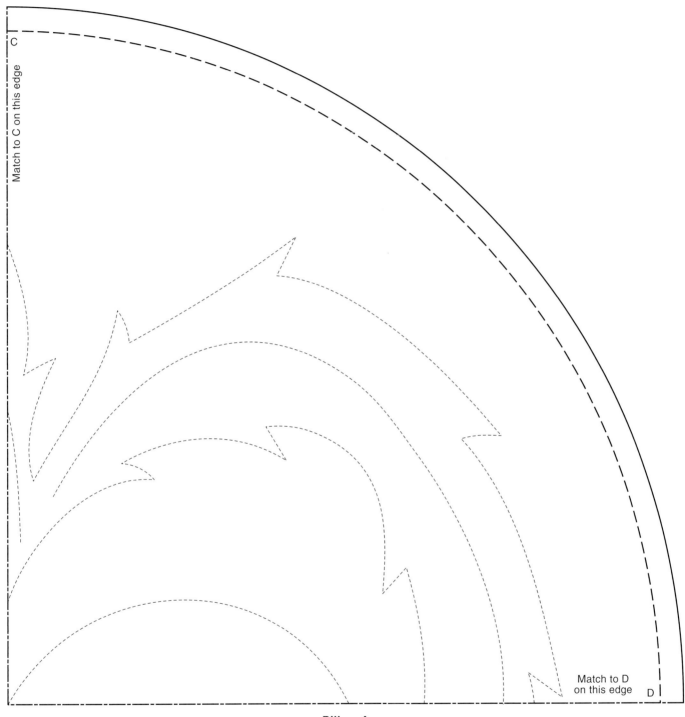

Match to C on this edge

C

Match to D
on this edge

D

Pillow 4

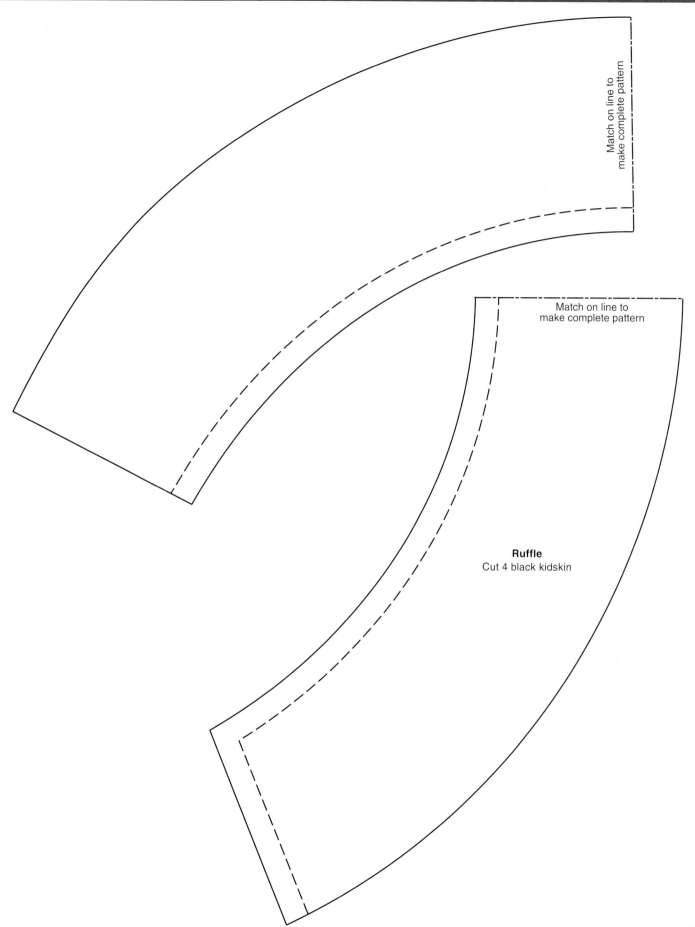

Match on line to make complete pattern

Match on line to
make complete pattern

Ruffle
Cut 4 black kidskin

Metric Conversion Charts

Metric Conversions

U.S. Measurements		Multiplied by		Metric Measurement
yards	x	.9144	=	meters (m)
yards	x	91.44	=	centimeters (cm)
inches	x	2.54	=	centimeters (cm)
inches	x	25.40	=	millimeters (mm)
inches	x	.0254	=	meters (m)

Metric Measurements		Multiplied by		U.S. Measurements
centimeters	x	.3937	=	inches
meters	x	1.0936	=	yards

Standard Equivalents

U.S. Measurement		Metric Measurement		
1/8 inch	=	3.20 mm	=	0.32 cm
1/4 inch	=	6.35 mm	=	0.635 cm
3/8 inch	=	9.50 mm	=	0.95 cm
1/2 inch	=	12.70 mm	=	1.27 cm
5/8 inch	=	15.90 mm	=	1.59 cm
3/4 inch	=	19.10 mm	=	1.91 cm
7/8 inch	=	22.20 mm	=	2.22 cm
1 inch	=	25.40 mm	=	2.54 cm
1/8 yard	=	11.43 cm	=	0.11 m
1/4 yard	=	22.86 cm	=	0.23 m
3/8 yard	=	34.29 cm	=	0.34 m
1/2 yard	=	45.72 cm	=	0.46 m
5/8 yard	=	57.15 cm	=	0.57 m
3/4 yard	=	68.58 cm	=	0.69 m
7/8 yard	=	80.00 cm	=	0.80 m
1 yard	=	91.44 cm	=	0.91 m

Resources

Leather
Tandy Leather Co.
(800) 433-3201
www.tandyleather.com

Batting
The batting listed is recommended for the quilts because it does not require close quilting, has a nice loft and stitches well.
Soft & Black
The Warm Co.
(800) 234-9276
www.warmcompany.com

Glue
Two types of glue are recommended, and the uses of each are noted in the General Instructions. The rubber cement is found in many shops. The basting glue is listed below.
Beacon's Quilter's Choice Basting Glue
Beacon Adhesives
(800) 865-7238
www.beaconcreates.com

Embroidery Stitch Guide

Buttonhole Stitch

French Knot

Lazy-Daisy Stitch

Cross-Stitch

Couching Stitch

Chevron Stitch

Satin Stitch

Herringbone Stitch

Stem Stitch

Fly Stitch

Feather-Stitches

Chain Stitch

Patricia Converse

A life-long love of nature inspires the work of designer Patricia Converse. She has written two quilt pattern books, *Inspired by Nature* and *Inspired by the Seasons,* currently being marketed by Leisure Arts. Creative Publishing is publishing two of Patricia's designs in the collaborative pattern book *When Quilter's Think Small.* She designs quilt kits and camera-ready patterns with instructions for her own distribution with Two in the Bush Designs.

Patricia's quilt designs include original and traditional patchwork and original appliqué. She also does paper cutting making original pieces inspired by traditional German/Swiss scherenschnitte. *PaperWorks* magazine has featured her work in the June and August 2004 issues. She has sold original handwoven wearable and home decorating works. She makes stained-glass commission pieces.

With a home economics degree from Keene State, part of the University of New Hampshire college system, Pat practiced her love for fabric in her classes emphasizing textiles and art. Dressmakers, sewing teachers and quilters in her family nurtured her love of sewing. She has worked briefly in many related areas: a design team member in the clothing industry, sewing teacher, dressmaker and fabric retailer. As an active volunteer in scouting and church, she has created and run children's crafts programs for 18 years. For 20 years she has worked as a secretary/bookkeeper. She lives and works at her country home in rural southern York County Pennsylvania.

Pat's goal is to enhance the love of art and craft through sharing her own with others.

E-mail: Customer_Service@whitebirches.com

HOUSE of WHITE BIRCHES
PUBLISHERS SINCE 1947

Learn to Quilt With Leather is published by House of White Birches, 306 East Parr Road, Berne, IN 46711, telephone (260) 589-4000. Printed in USA. Copyright © 2005 House of White Birches.

RETAILERS: If you would like to carry this pattern book or any other House of White Birches publications, call the Wholesale Department at Annie's Attic to set up a direct account: (903) 636-4303. Also, request a complete listing of publications available from House of White Birches.

Every effort has been made to ensure that the instructions in this pattern book are complete and accurate. We cannot, however, take responsibility for human error, typographical mistakes or variations in individual work.

ISBN: 1-59217-061-7
1 2 3 4 5 6 7 8 9

STAFF
Editors: Jeanne Stauffer, Sandra L. Hatch
Associate Editor: Dianne Schmidt
Technical Artist: Connie Rand
Copy Supervisor: Michelle Beck
Copy Editors: Conor Allen, Sue Harvey, Nicki Lehman

Graphic Arts Supervisor: Ronda Bechinski
Graphic Artists: Erin Augsburger, Joanne Gonzalez
Assistant Art Director: Karen Allen
Photography: Tammy Christian, Carl Clark, Christena Green and Matt Owen
Photo Stylist: Tammy Nussbaum